teach me about

Friends

Managing Editor: Ellen Klarberg
Copy Editor: Kate Dickey
Contributing Writer: Kathleen McBride
Contributing Editors: Libby Byers, Maureen Dryden, Yona Flemming
Consultant: Richard Camp, D.V.M., M.S.
Donald Meyer, M.D., Roger Pitzen, M.D.
Editorial Assistant: Sandy Passarino

Art Director: Laurie Westdahl
Design and Production: Abigail Johnston
Illustrator: Bartholomew
Inker: Susie Hornig
Production Assistant: Lillian Cram
Composition: Curt Chelin

teach me about

Friends

By JOY BERRY

Illustrated by Bartholomew

GROLIER ENTERPRISES CORP.

Sometimes a friend comes to my house. We play with the toys that are at my house. There are some toys that I do not want my friend to play with. I put these toys away before my friend comes. I do not play with them while my friend is at my house.

Sometimes I go to a friend's house. We play with the toys that are at my friend's house.

There are some toys that my friend does not want me to play with.

I do not play with them.

I ask if it is OK before I play

with my friend's toys.

I play carefully with my

friend's toys so that

I will not break them.

I put the toys away when I am

finished using them.

Sometimes I meet my friend at school. We play with the toys that are at school. Other times I meet my friend at a special place. We both bring toys to play with.

Sometimes my friend and I want to play with the same toy at the same time. I do not want to fight with my friend. I let my friend play with the toy first. I play with the toy when my friend is finished playing with it.

Sometimes my friend does

not give me a chance

to play with a toy.

I tell my friend that

it is my turn

to play with the toy.

Sometimes my friend says,

"You cannot have a turn

playing with this toy."

I ask a big person to talk to

my friend.

The big person reminds my

friend that I need to have

a turn to play with the toy.

It is best when my friend and I take turns deciding what we are going to do.

First we do what my friend wants to do.

Then we do what I want to do.

It is best when my friend and I are kind to each other.

It is best when we do not say or do mean things to each other.

Sometimes my friend

gets mad at me

and tries to hurt me.

I tell my friend,

"I do not like that!

Please stop it!"

Sometimes my friend

does not stop hurting me

when I say, "Please stop it!"

When this happens,

I go away from my friend.

Sometimes my friend

follows me and

still tries to hurt me

when I go away.

I ask a big person to help me.

The big person stops my

friend from hurting me.

Sometimes my friend does

something that makes me angry.

I tell my friend,

"You are making me angry.

Please stop it!"

Sometimes my friend does

not stop making me angry.

When this happens,

I go away from my friend.

I do not play with friends
who are not being fair.
I do not play with friends
who are being mean and
trying to hurt me.

My friend and I are

kind to each other.

We have fun when we are

together.

helpful hints for parents about

Friends

Dear Parents:

The purpose of this book is

- to prepare children for social interaction with peers by teaching them what to expect and how to behave when they are with friends, and
- to empower children with the right to select friends and the right to walk away if they are not pleased with what is happening to them in play situations.

You can best implement the purpose of this book by

- reading it to your child, and
- reading the following *Helpful Hints* and using them whenever applicable.

FRIENDSHIP

Lifelong friendships can be the happy result of your child's earliest social contacts. Parents are the key to early friendships because they create the opportunities for children to establish important bonds outside the family.

Value of a peer group

Parents are rewarded with a new perspective on their child when they see him or her with peers in the early stages of establishing a social identity. The separation of parent and child when the child is with friends encourages the process of healthy separation which is the end product of successful parenting.

General information about toddler friendships:

- Babies are more attracted to persons their own age and size than to adults.
- Young children will generally choose another child to play with over any toy.
- Peers are often the most effective teachers of social skills.
- A playmate's size and physical and mental abilities are more significant for a toddler friendship than the playmate's age.
- Toddler interaction involves some pushing and shoving that requires a certain amount of physical matching.

Peer group options

By the age of 18 months your child will probably want to make regular contact with other children. You can arrange for your child to be with other children in any of the following ways:

- Arrange to meet with other parents and their children at a park or playground.
- Exchange child care with another parent whose child is compatible with your child and close to the same age.
- Organize a regular play group in your home.

- Enroll your child (age 3 or older) in a nursery school or child care facility.
- Investigate community sponsored programs for young children, such as
    parent-child gymnastics,
    swimming classes,
    day camps, and
    library story hours.

ORGANIZING PEER GROUP EXPERIENCES

Casual arrangements by parents to meet at a park or playground can provide peer group contact and add variety to a young child's daily routine. This activity works especially well with one- to two-year-olds who may enjoy the company of another child for up to an hour.

Child care exchanges offer your child the opportunity for one-to-one playtime with a friend in your home or theirs. Choose parents for this arrangement whose child-rearing philosophy is compatible with yours and who can be trusted with the care of your child in the exchange. Playmates need to be reasonably compatible as well.

Play groups seem to work well for parents and their children under age three. No program or structuring of the routine is required, but organization is essential. Parents take turns supervising their child's playmates at home on a rotating schedule.

Consider the following guidelines when organizing a play group:
- Recruit reliable parents willing to carry their share of the responsibilities for the play group.
- Be fair in reciprocal exchanges of child supervision. Parents resent any imbalance and may unconsciously project their resentment onto your child rather than speaking to you about it.
- Limit the ratio of participating children to four for each supervising adult.
- Plan to meet two days a week for no more than two hours a day.
- Rotate play sessions among the participating households.

Establish health and safety guidelines for the play group.
Gather information on allergies, medications, preferred first-aid treatment, emergency procedures, and emergency telephone numbers for each child.
Prepare snacks, drinks, and the play environment ahead of time.
Supply a variety of toys such as puzzles, plastic containers, push/pull toys, small vehicles, edible play dough, books, and records or cassettes. You don't need a toy store, just enough items to go around to minimize the need for sharing.
Supervise the play group at all times.

PLAY EXPERIENCES

Very young children seldom play together, but rather side by side in parallel activities.

Your expectations

Do not expect your child under three
- to share his or her toys, or
- to interact positively with a playmate.

You can encourage the development of these social skills in the following ways:
- Have your child's playmates bring one or two of their own toys with them to your home. Two-way sharing or trading is easier than one-way sharing.
- Allow your child to offer the snacks you provide to young visitors. Be sure there are plenty to go around and try to keep sizes uniform.
- Provide some treats or small toys previously packaged and labeled with each child's name. These special items do not require sharing.
- When something whole is being divided for sharing, have one child do the dividing and another the choosing.
- Encourage your child to show visitors how and where to properly use any special toys that are being shared.
- Put away any toys you or your child do not wish to share.

- Use a timer for sharing one item among two or more children.
- Allow children to work out their own conflicts as far as possible. Negative physical contact, however, demands immediate interaction.
- Assume an objective adult role in your child's relationships with friends. Try not to take sides, hold grudges, or penalize unfairly when intervention in a conflict is necessary.
- Help children in conflict to communicate their problems verbally to one another. This type of conflict resolution requires an adult facilitator to help children verbalize.
- Make sure there is adequate stimulation. Misbehavior in children is generally due to boredom (a lack of stimulation) which can be destructive and dangerous if not redirected into stimulating activity.
- Do not force friendships with children for whom your child expresses a dislike.

PRESCHOOLS

Most preschools have age and developmental requirements for enrollment. Generally, preschools require that children be two years nine months of age and toilet trained. Child care centers also offer peer group opportunities for young children with minimal requirements for enrollment. Parents who do not require full- or part-time child care may choose from a variety of preschool options for their child including
- private or church affiliated nursery schools
- parent cooperative nursery schools
- Montessori schools
- Waldorf schools
- Head Start programs
- university or college sponsored nursery schools

Choosing a preschool
Apply the following guidelines in choosing a preschool:

- Consider only licensed preschools. The state license should be displayed, or you can ask to see it.
- Begin your preschool evaluation and selection process well in advance of your child's planned enrollment to avoid waiting lists or a hasty decision.
- Ask for recommendations from other parents whose judgment you trust.
- Look for a government published directory of preschools in your community. Local child advocacy groups often distribute such publications.
- Make a list of possible selections based on recommendations you have obtained.
- Arrange to observe the schools on your list, and talk to the teachers without your child. Ask to meet all employees and volunteers at the school.
- Be sure you understand and agree with the educational philosophy of a potential choice.
- Consider the school's distance from your home and your transportation needs.
- Be willing to pay what you can reasonably afford when cost is relative to the quality of the program.

Monitoring your child's preschool

Once your child is enrolled in a preschool you will want to be sure the program and staff meet your expectations for quality. Your child's behavior is the best indicator of problems or satisfaction with his or her preschool experience. Watch for the following signs which may indicate a negative preschool experience or problems with separating from parents:
- continued protest about going to preschool;
- anxious waiting for your return and requests to leave immediately;
- increased dependency behavior at home;
- withdrawal or regressive behavior such as thumb-sucking, bed-wetting, or return to bottles when such behavior has been outgrown.

Your child's preschool experience is a positive one when his or her behavior indicates:
- increased independence and confidence;
- willingness to try new experiences;
- ability to separate from parents for longer periods of time;
- improvement in ability to get along with playmates;
- happy anticipation of going to preschool and of the activities there.

How to monitor your child's preschool

Your child's preschool can be observed and evaluated by you in any of the following ways:
- Stay awhile occasionally when you drop off your child for school.
- Make regular appointments to talk with the teacher about your child and the program.
- Pick up your child earlier than usual from time to time.
- Pay surprise visits to the preschool occasionally, without being disruptive to the program.
- Check with any parents whose child drops out of the nursery school to be sure their choice did not involve dissatisfaction with the school.
- Consult regularly with other parents of children in the school to share observations and evaluations.

If your negative evaluation of the school warrants removing your child, the preschool should be reported to the proper authorities to spare other children possible harm. Your positive evaluation of your child's preschool experience should be expressed, preferably in writing, to teachers and their supervisors.